The world is fo [barcode: C000075456]
as well as to ...

To dear friends
Trevor & Shaler

Chengde
17/12/2001 Oxford

Five Themes of Today
Philosophical Poems

by Chengde Chen

OPEN GATE PRESS
incorporating Centaur Press
LONDON

First published in 2001 by Open Gate Press
51 Achilles Road, London NW6 1DZ

British Library Cataloguing-in-Publication Programme
A catalogue reference for this book is available from the
British Library.

ISBN: 1 871871 54 9

Produced by Bookchase (UK) Ltd

To Those Who Think

Someone said that when man thinks, God laughs
But if man does not think, God will be bored
God likes the fun of thinking but not its hard work
So He creates man to do the work for Him
Man has two options:
to think – to be a hard-working God
not to think – to be a relaxed slave
This oldest of Greek issues about thinking
is still the first issue that needs to be thought

— On Thinking

Contents

Appendices

Foreword

The poems of the present collection have a somewhat unusual character. They could be called *philosophical poems* in that each poem contains philosophical arguments given in a poetic form. It is perhaps no surprising that their author, Chengde Chen, started as a professional philosopher. He was an associate professor of philosophy in Shanghai in the 1980s with a particular interest in the philosophy of Karl Popper. Chen left China in 1989 and continued studying philosophy for a while at Oxford University. During this period he wrote a paper called 'Asymmetrical Thinking' in which he developed some ideas of Popper's. Popper makes the point that looking at things from the negative side often gives a different perspective from the positive side. The ethical theory of Utilitarianism provides a good example of this. The theory is normally formulated in a positive sense by saying that it is good to promote the largest possible sum of human happiness. However Popper suggested that we might consider instead the project of reducing to its lowest possible level the sum of human misery. This negative formulation gives a different way of looking at the problem. In his paper Chen builds on this and other examples of Popper's to produce a general logical account of looking at things from the negative as opposed to positive side. I studied under Popper as a graduate student many years ago, and when Chen's paper fell into my hands, I found it very interesting. This is what led to our meeting.

It was a year or so after we had become friendly that Chen moved from doing philosophy in the standard way to writing his philosophical poems. It seems at first sight most curious to present a philosophical argument in the form of a poem, but when one examines the matter historically, it turns out that there are a few precedents. In ancient Greek times, for example, the pre-Socratic philosopher Parmenides wrote his main philosophical work on the Way of Truth and the Way of Seeming in the form of a poem, *On Nature*. The poem actually begins as follows:

> The steeds that carry me took me as far as my heart could desire, when once they had brought me and set me on the renowned way of the goddess, who leads the man who knows through every town. On that way was I conveyed; for on it did the wise steeds convey me, drawing my chariot, and maidens led the way.

After this opening, which is poetic in the conventional sense, the reader may be surprised to be plunged into one of the densest logical arguments to be found in any work of philosophy. The model for Western philosophers, however, was not Parmenides' poem, but the surviving works of Aristotle, which led to the typically dry and quite unpoetic philosophical treatise.

Moving closer to our own time, T.S. Eliot is a poet who could be considered philosophical. Indeed Eliot was a graduate student of Bertrand Russell's when Russell was lecturing at Harvard. Eliot continued to study philosophy both at Harvard and Oxford, and finished a doctoral thesis at Harvard. Although he remained friendly with Russell, he disagreed with his philosophy, and espoused instead the absolute idealism of Russell's opponent Bradley. Bradley's philosophy was very metaphysical in character, and one finds metaphysical reflections in some of Eliot's poems. A famous example is the opening of *Burnt Norton*, the first of the *Four Quartets*.

> Time present and time past
> Are both perhaps present in time future,
> And time future contained in time past.
> If all time is eternally present
> All time is unredeemable.

What might have been is an abstraction
Remaining a perpetual possibility
Only in a world of speculation.

It is important to emphasise that the sense in which Chen's poems
are philosophical is not this metaphysical sense. Chen emphasises
the other side of philosophy, its argumentative quality. His poems
contain sustained pieces of argumentation. In this sense Chen's
philosophy is closer to that of Russell than to that of the metaphysical Bradley. Indeed his poem 'On the Logic of Love and
Marriage' contains an extensive discussion of Russell's ideas on
this subject.

But is there any advantage in working philosophical arguments
into poems? I believe that there is, and will now explain why. In
the poetry of the past, narrative poems played a large role. Both
epics and popular ballads fell into this category. This had the
advantage that the adventures of the hero, whether Odysseus, Sir
Patrick Spens, or Thomas the Rhymer, provided an interest and a
forward drive, moving the reader or listener on through the poem.
The same momentum is to be found in verse drama, but it can be
lacking in lyrical poems, which all too often express a static mood
and feeling. There is thus a danger of stagnation and even boredom
in the lyrical poem. In our modern world, the narrative poem and
also verse drama have largely been abandoned. So we are left with
mood poems and the risk of dullness.

Chen's philosophical poems offer a way out of this difficulty.
In his verses the forward movement of a narrative is replaced by
the forward movement of an argument. It is these challenging
arguments which carry the reader along, and sustain the interest.
Whatever other faults Chen may have, he is never dull, and I can
guarantee that most readers will find his collection gripping from
beginning to end.

The interest of Chen's poems is increased by the fact that his
philosophy is not abstract and remote, but related to everyday
problems with which we are all faced. Probably his most striking
poem is 'On the End of Technological Civilisation' which argues
that our type of society based on science and technology will not
be able to sustain itself for any length of time. This is an unwelcome

conclusion for admirers of science and technology such as myself, but Chen uses all his skill as a philosopher to make his case, and it is difficult to fault his arguments. The philosophical ideas derived from Popper which I mentioned earlier are brought in at one point:

> This plain and simple fact
> shows how the negative can count more than the positive
> So it is with our technological civilisation
> Technological progress, no matter how often it happens
> can only be partial and limited
> Technological catastrophe, no matter how rarely it happens
> can be full-scale and thorough
> Construction is a process, while destruction is a conclusion –
> ten thousand years of achievements can be destroyed in a
> > second

Each of Chen's poems deals with an important contemporary theme: love and marriage, reason and religion, liberty and equality, democracy. His arguments challenge us to think more deeply about the problems facing humanity.

Chen has lived in both China and England. His poems are appearing in Chinese as well as in English. He thus has an international perspective well suited to the contemporary globalisation of human society. This invites one further reflection. Is the new genre of the philosophical poem which is here introduced suited to the emergence of an international literature? Could it be that while moods and narratives are more local and national, philosophical arguments can touch issues which are more universal and hence important for all the members of the new global community? If this is so, then the philosophical poem may be destined to become an established genre. But whatever the future holds in this respect, the reader will certainly find this collection of poems enjoyable and thought-provoking.

Donald Gillies
Professor of Philosophy
King's College, London

Acknowledgements

Some works in this collection have been published or accepted by literary and philosophical journals in English and Chinese. I would like to thank these publications for supporting my rather unconventional writings: *The Guardian* (UK), *Hong Kong Literature* (HK), *ENVOI* (UK), *Poetry Monthly* (UK), *Acumen* (UK), *The Selected Works of Taiwan & Hong Kong Literature* (P. R. China), *The Philosopher* (UK), *New Analysis* (UK), *Philosophy and Culture* (Taiwan), *Panorama Monthly* (P.R.China). I also thank Oxford's 'Back Room Poets', Wadham College's 'Wadham Poetry Evening', and 'Poetic Licence' for various poetry readings they organised, which have shown that philosophical poems can be understood and welcomed through reading poetry.

I wholeheartedly thank:

Dr John Rutherford, for all his help during the last ten years, at both Queen's College, his friendly home, and his 'Conference Centre'. He it is that has taught me to understand and respect England and her people;

Dwight Middleton, Mary and David Ormerod, for correcting my English in almost all my writings – without such help none of my work would have reached its present state; great language barriers can be overcome even in philosophy and poetry, but you need very good friends to do so;

Prof. Donald Gillies, for his academic inspiration and support, which cannot be expected from anyone else; thus I should also thank Karl Popper for his destined 'introduction' to this precious friendship;

Geoff Mills and Susan Coxhead, for all their kindness and invaluable support which can only be explained by true friendship;

Bernard Donoghue, for his literary advice and comments on my works, which tells me that philosophical poems can be appreciated by distinguished poets;

The late Vernon Futerman, for his understanding of my work and effective publishing advice;

Prof. Fengsheng Guo, for all his comments and invaluable help in and from China, which has kept me in touch with both worlds rather than missing one of them;

Yichang Liu, for his courage in supporting my unconventional writings in his prestigious publication so that they have reached readers in Hong Kong and mainland China;

The Queen's College, University of Oxford, for continuously supporting my academic work for many years;

Jeannie Cohen, Sandra Lovell, and Open Gate Press, for their appreciation of my work, as well as their efforts and professionalism towards the publication of this collection.

I am also grateful to the following people who have supported me in writing this collection of philosophical poems: Tita Rutherford, Roberta Middleton, Joan Coxhead, Jonathan Cohen, Rom Harre, John Hyman, Gino Russo, Alison Deer, Heather Bradshaw, Emma Bonner-Morgan, Jason Bentsman, Rip Bulkeley, Ian Warrand, Martin and Margrate, David Bliss, Qi Qiu, Le Chen, Chenghui Chen, Shengyan Fan, Qing Yu, Zhengya Shen, Hui Huang, Yun Xie, Changwen Shen, and Mingxian Shen.

Finally, I would like to express my gratitude to my parents Yanti Chen and Yi Shen, who have always been there for me, as well as to the following friends: Weihang Chen, Mingfeng Shan, Jinmin Zhang, Derek and Maria Dean, Tim O'Hagan, Angus Ross, Charles Boyle, and Nicola Macbean.

Chengde Chen
Queen's College
University of Oxford
October 2001

I. Five Themes of Today

On the End of Technological Civilisation
The Mathematics and Philosophy of Self-destruction

'Men live in fear of destruction by the atom bomb or biological weapon; in hope of living better lives through the application of science in agriculture and medicine'

J. D. Bernal's *Science in History*

Argument

Mathematics tells that an accelerating process cannot last, as an infinite speed is impossible. Technological development is an accelerating process, so it will end. How will this happen? Technological advances, such as nuclear technology, genetic engineering, etc., have developed the capability, and thus the possibility, to destroy civilisation. The growth of possibility is the rise of probability, which will eventually mature into reality in the river of time – 'the Car-crash Theory' (Chapter 5) has proved the inevitability of such self-destruction. The only way to avoid it happening is to abandon the utilitarian value system that pursues technological development, so as to replace technological civilisation with an artistic civilisation. Art will not accelerate, as it is not a function of time.

1. Prologue

There may be many kinds of civilisation
but mathematically speaking, there are only two –
those that understand mathematics and those that don't
Those that do may not last as long as mathematics
but those that don't will be destroyed by the law of
    mathematics
Unfortunately, our technological civilisation belongs to the
        latter
More unfortunately, mankind has not realised this at all!

2. Technological Civilisation's Mathematical Problem

We call our civilisation a 'technological civilisation'
because technology is its origin and development
Since the whistle of the Industrial Revolution
broke the calm of agricultural civilisation
mankind has realised how best to exploit its potential
Human beings are intelligent
Human beings are competitive
The intelligence of competition is the MARKET
The competition of intelligence is TECHNOLOGY

From the day that the steam engine changed old social
          structures
– large industries transformed peasants as well as land
till today the computer is creating a new way of life
– raising man's head for the second time since he stood up
(writing with computers we no longer bend over our desks!)
the 200 years of technological advance have shown that
there is nothing technology cannot do
It is the profit of capital, and also the capital of profit
It is the source of wealth, and also the cause of revolution
It is the answer to all problems, and also where all hopes lie
It is a visible and tangible 'God' – worshipped by the world
Even that invisible One is forming a 'joint venture' with it:
churches are spreading the Gospel on the Internet
believers are e-mailing their prayers to Heaven . . .

However, technological advance is an accelerating process
It runs faster, and faster, and faster

It took 100,000 years from rolling trees to inventing the wheel
It took 10,000 years from the wheel to the locomotive
While it only took 100 years from the locomotive to the
          spacecraft
Technological developments over the last 200 years
have been more than those of the previous 2000
Technological innovations over the last 50 years
have been more than those of the previous 200

Scientific studies of the history of science and technology
(best done by D. J. Price* and J. D. Bernal†) show that
knowledge and technology are an accelerating system
in the sense that, generally
the rate of their growth follows 'the exponential rule'
The causes of this are:
(a) mankind pursues knowledge and technology
(b) knowledge and technology are cumulative

As far as nature is concerned, the human race is a monster
Any natural system that has its birth must have its death
except the human race, which does not die
because its knowledge does not die –
Confucius' thoughts are still alive in the East
Plato's 'ideas' are still alive in the West
The handing down of knowledge makes 'human death' an
          illusion
The development of knowledge accumulates technological
          power

---

* D. J. Price's *Little Science, Big Science*, New York, 1963
† J. D. Bernal's *Science in History*, The MIT Press,1974 (p.676): 'As Price has shown,
the exponential rule applies very exactly to knowledge itself, measured by number of
papers published; the present scientific revolution being marked by a doubling every ten
years. Price's conclusion that this cannot go on until everyone is a scientist is certainly
true.'

Accumulation leads to acceleration:
the larger its foundation, the faster it develops –
exponentially as bacteria breeding

Now we are in a so-called information age, which means
technological progress has reached a chain reaction
with the speed of electricity
The expansion of knowledge causes the explosion of human
        activity
The explosion of activity causes the further expansion of
        knowledge
This is not two madnesses encountering each other by chance
but a destined mutual escalation between raging fire and the
        wind

Everyone regards this as just what we desire
Everyone is trying to make the racehorse faster –
investing more in scientific education
speeding up research and development
so as to gain more benefit and profit

No one, however, has ever noticed that
mathematically, there is a question to be answered:
if speed cannot increase infinitely
how can an accelerating system last?

It seems merely an imaginary question
which no one would regard as a 'question'
but its logic is as clear as that night follows day
Could this great civilisation, of which we are so proud
have been a wild horse running towards the edge of a cliff
where there are no stop-signs?
Let's hope we still have time to understand the problem
before it is too late even to regret

3. Acceleration and Collapsing

Mathematics says:
no accelerating system can last
because an infinite speed is impossible
Physically, an 'infinite speed' means transcendence
i.e., taking no time to travel from one place to another
i.e., being at two places at the same time
which cannot happen
In fact, any accelerating process in nature
ends in some form of collapse

A free-falling body is an accelerating process –
it soon ends in a crash
A nuclear reaction is an accelerating process –
it quickly perishes together with its environment
The accelerating splitting of cells is called cancer –
it rapidly destroys life
No matter what process it is –
physical, chemical, or biological
all have to obey the law of mathematics
This is why Pythagoras says 'all things are numbers'

There is no exception
as it is impossible to have any exceptions
including the system of knowledge and technology
which looks like an exception
That is to say, if mathematical law is a law
it is impossible for this system to last
If we have the slightest measure of reason
how can we argue with mathematics?

Technology may be, as some say, 'an expression of reason'
but collapsing is the logical implication of acceleration –
although it is difficult to imagine
how this 'invincible' civilisation will collapse in all its glory!

With regard to how civilisation may end
there seems to be various possibilities
But, if an end is concluded from the logic that
no accelerating development can last
it would have to be caused by such development itself
Therefore, the question becomes:
how would development lead to an end?

Despite originating from logical inference
the question cannot be answered through logical derivation
Just as from the proposition 'all men die'
logic can conclude that Socrates would die
but not how he would
To assess how development may lead to an end
is to establish two things based on empirical facts:
(a) real possibilities for technology to finish civilisation
(b) the inevitability of such possibilities turning into reality

4. Civilisation's Capability to Destroy Itself

In the great Twentieth Century
technological advance reached an unprecedented level
However, what distinguishes it in history
is neither space travel, nor optical communication
nor artificial intelligence, nor genetic engineering
but that it has reached an unprecedented capability:
it can destroy itself!

Before, the human race had no such capability
The only force that could destroy civilisation was that of nature
such as an ice age or a crustal movement

Now, we can do it ourselves
Nuclear technology is the first indisputable possibility
This great discovery of releasing energy from atomic nuclei
immediately reduced the security coefficient of mankind to
          zero
Today, the number of nuclear warheads the world possesses
is capable of destroying our civilisation twenty times over
Everything man has built over tens of thousands of years
lies in the few-millimetre gap between two contact points
of a nuclear button!

It is merely luck that we have not been destroyed
By chance Hitler's actions were a little bit slow
By chance the temperature of the Cold War was a little bit low
Undoubtedly, we have had the capability of destroying
          ourselves
which is something we shouldn't be modest about
– No, we shouldn't!

Self-destruction has become a magnificent possibility
This is an epoch-making milestone of technological
     civilisation

Not only nuclear technology
the possibilities of destruction are developing in many
          directions

Genetic engineering is breaking the boundaries between species
while viruses crossing barriers could give mankind a fatal blow

Spaceships are hospitably inviting outside civilisations
while our guests could be merciless giants
who like to have 'fried human ants' for dinner!
(Sounds like some 'size horror', but what would the fact that
the Earth, diameter-wise, is only one per cent of the Sun tell
          us?)

Artificial intelligence is providing machines with our brains
while it is not impossible for robots to develop an 'ethic'
advocating machine-revolution to destroy their creators!

We can never know the consequences of technology
just as scientists, by definition, can never be God!
Technological advance means bringing us new things
Our limited experiments would never be sufficient to assess
their possible interaction with the rest of the world
and their long-term consequences

We had been friends of plastic for over half of a century
and applied it to nearly every aspect of our lives
until it was suddenly discovered that male fish were laying eggs
and men's sperm count was falling dramatically
we then found that it is oestrogen's ally rather than ours

We had enjoyed refrigerant technology for over fifty years
using the easy-going freon to obtain desired temperatures
until a large hole was discovered above the South Pole
and skin cancer in Australia rose rapidly
we then noticed this fellow was greedily swallowing ozone
– the defence force protecting us from ultraviolet radiation

Today, the British turn pale at the mention of beef
scared that mad cow disease could cause mad men
But, didn't the disaster result from the new feeding-technology
– feeding herbivores with meat to increase animal protein?
If cows could speak, they would ask Heaven for justice:
how could there be mad cows, if there were no mad men?
(However, some say it might have been too late even for men –
for this burger-loving nation – to realise this anyway
as the incubation period for CJD could be as long as thirty
          years!)

The consequences of technology are endless – beyond
          prediction
The only thing that is predictable is its unpredictability
as well as the possibility of various disasters
The development of possibility is the rise of probability
Probability will mature into reality in the river of time

5. *'The Car-crash Theory' and Popper's Philosophy*

When technology is capable of destroying civilisation
its development is laying mines
When the density of the minefield reaches a certain degree
destruction becomes no longer a question of 'if'
but 'when' it will happen
If it does not take this form, it will take another form
If it does not happen this time, it will happen next time!

It is argued that
although there are risks in technological progress
the pros are much greater than the cons
Is this so?
No
Since man has been capable of destroying himself
this argument has lost its grounds
What can we do in the ashes of nuclear destruction –
appreciate the wonder of laser music
or enjoy the comfort of a new-model car?
You may say the possibility of such catastrophes is very very
            small
but the time span of the existence of mankind is very very large
I have a simple analysis called 'the car-crash theory'
which proves the inevitability of the self-destruction
and so the great asymmetry between the pros and cons

Assuming a man could have eternal life, in which
the only possible death were by a car-crash when he drove

and if he wished to live forever
should he drive or not?

We all know that there are benefits and risks in driving
We decide to take the risks
not only because we like the benefits
but also because our lives are limited
It is very possible to drive throughout life without a crash
as our lives last only several decades
Whereas, for a person who could have eternal life
driving would amount to committing suicide
because the probability of driving a million years without a
        crash
is almost zero
Therefore, if he were a man of reason
he should not drive

Mankind is such a 'man'
and technological development is his 'car'
Yes, tremendous enjoyment and excitement
but a fatal accident is only a matter of time
While, we are so irrational, almost laughable
We make a great fuss over an individual death
but take no notice of the suicide of mankind as a whole!
Someone says a probability is merely a probability
but, isn't it worse
to commit suicide with probability than with rope?
Sudden death gives no time to arrange one's affairs

There was a philosopher called Karl Popper
who proposed a theory called Falsificationism
It says there is asymmetry between proof and disproof
For example, by seeing thousands of white swans

we do not prove the proposition that 'all swans are white'
but by seeing one black swan
we have disproved this proposition categorically
This plain and simple fact
shows how the negative can count more than the positive

So it is with our technological civilisation
Technological progress, no matter how often it happens
can be only partial and limited
Technological catastrophe, no matter how rare it happens
can be full-scale and thorough
Construction is a process, while destruction is a conclusion
Ten thousand years of achievements can be destroyed in a
          second
Therefore, since mankind has been capable of destroying itself
the cons of technological progress have far outweighed the
          pros!

When good climbs an inch, evil climbs a foot
The greater our intelligence, the more dangerous it becomes
If the nature of technology is to accumulate power of
          destruction
then the meaning of civilisation is to accelerate towards its
          end
Mankind
please see your absurdity through the lens of mathematics
The progress we are making is a process of self-destruction
The luxuries we are enjoying are arts of euthanasia
The respectable forces of science are grave-diggers of
          civilisation
The noble Nobel Prizes are gravestones without future
          generations to tend them!

6. The Non-linear Mathematics of History

Things are so obvious, but why can't we see them?
We are still obsessed with developing technology
as if we wished to hasten our destruction
This is because history is deceptive
We have no understanding of the mathematics of history
and are immersed in a linear perception of 'progress'
We believe that history has proved man controls technology
and history has proved technology does more good than harm
This seems our unshakeable faith
as it is the experience of thousands of years

We, of course, need to rely on history
which is the only thing that we have
History, however, is not a piece of repeatable music
but non-linear mathematics
Some histories are mirrors of futures
while some futures have no reflection of history at all
It is very difficult to establish this non-linear understanding
as such an understanding is very different from our intuition
It is because of such a difficulty that, as a famous story relates
Dahir, an Indian wise man of 3000 years ago
nearly made the King give up his Kingdom

One day, the chess-loving King challenged Dahir
by asking him to play the final phase of a losing battle
He promised, with the authority of a King
'if you win, you are entitled to make a request of any kind'
Dahir did win, with his superior intelligence
However, he only made a very small request

'I would like to have some grain
placed on the chessboard in the following way:
one for the first square
two for the second
four for the third, and so on
That is the grain for each square is twice that of the previous
      one
till all 64 squares of the chessboard are placed'

What an insignificant request, the King thought
and approved it immediately
He ordered his soldiers to bring in a sack of grain
When one sack had been finished, another was served
Then another, and another . . .
until they exhausted all the grain in the Kingdom
it was still far from completing the 64 squares
2^{63} is an astronomical figure beyond imagination
Even the amount of grain in today's world
does not come near it (1000 billion tonne)!
While those small figures at the start
as well as the linear perception of that history
made the wise King miscalculate completely
and he is still in debt to Dahir to this day

This is also our mathematics of history
except that the curve of technological progress is more
      deceptive
It crawled slowly during ancient history
while it has risen sharply after the Industrial Revolution
The thousands of years, however, gave the impression of
      'history'
so the future was imagined as its 'mirror image'

People believe that
as man has progressed from the past through technology
through it he can, of course, progress towards the future
as technology has become more and more powerful
man will, of course, become more and more capable

Oh, the wishful thinking of mathematical ignoramuses!
History is not optics
nor is the future a mirror image of the past
In the past man was only a small member of the kingdom of
        nature
while today we have changed the weather, raised oceans
and created new species as well as new forms of energy
If we cannot see such a world of difference
we are miscalculating as the old King did

We cannot, however, afford to miscalculate
as we would have no time even to be surprised
The surface value of history is its usefulness for us
but the deeper value of history is to prove itself useless
The history in which we controlled technology was only history
No matter how brilliant it was
the future means a ruthless breaking away from history!

7. *The Answer to the Riddle of Needs*

People have always believed that
it is a human need to develop technology
but this is a confusion of two kinds of needs –
needs for survival and needs of a value system
The former comes from nature
while the latter is created by man
If we chose a different value system
then we would 'need' different things

Developing technology was originally a need for man to
       survive
From drilling wood for fire, to farming and weaving
man needed to claim his fill, warmth, and security from nature
In the great struggle for survival
we formed a utilitarian value system –
pursuing wealth and advocating competition
with the market and technology as its two engines
This value system drove the economy successfully
and then the economy meant survival

It is because this system has been so successful
that it has become the soul guiding our thinking
What else do we need after meeting the needs for survival?
No one knows, as the answer is something to be created
The utilitarian values are the creators –
Technology tells us what we 'can' need
The market tells us what we 'do' need

Originally we did not need the car
but since the car was invented and on the market
we came to need it

and need it so much that we would feel imprisoned without it
Originally we did not need the television
but since the television was invented and on the market
we came to need it
and need it so much that we would feel our day incomplete
          without it

. . .

Modern society is a technology-addicted society
Technology for us is spirits, nicotine, cocaine for the addicts
It creates the blood and nerves that need it, as well as
the greed for material goods and the desire for competition

Do we need air travel?
Do we need to fly at the speed of a bullet?
Why is travelling to a remote and strange continent
more enjoyable than visiting neighbours or friends nearby?
Do we need to go to the Moon?
Do we need to be a hero of destroying its beautiful fairy-tales?
Why is a lunar crater, dead for a million years, more interesting
than the green hills and flowing rivers of our homeland?
Do we need those medicines for prolonging life?
Do we need to live in the electric current of a life-support
          machine?
Why is letting a withered leaf struggle on a winter's branch
more moral or more sensible than allowing it to go naturally?

We do not 'need' them, but we think we do
It is because of nothing but competition –
because we are 'able to' or 'not able to':
we need to be able to do what others are able to do
as well as what others are not able to do
If you are able to fly into space, I must be able to touch the
          Moon

If you have landed on Venus first, I must visit Mars first
even though millions of hungry children are crying on Earth!

It has always been believed that life needs competition
but, in fact, it is competition that makes the need for
          competition
The strong swagger around, and the weak refuse to be outdone
Those in the middle are struggling against both ends
Every one is forcing others to be competitors
Every nation is forcing other nations to be opponents
Oh, why is this necessary?
Once escaping from the utilitarian net
you will see this world war is no more than a game
As the Chinese say:
if no side wants to win a war
they win the peace together!

Indeed, many of our needs are not 'our' needs
but the needs of our values
The answer to the riddle of needs lies in our value system
The utilitarian system, however, is only one of the possible
          systems
Although it championed civilisation, it is not a law for eternity
nor is it the unique way offered by Heaven and Earth
If the danger of self-destruction means a new need for
          survival
mankind will have to choose a new system

8. The Option of an Artistic Civilisation

The problem of technological civilisation destroying itself
cannot be solved within technological civilisation
It is not an environmental problem that concerns
      environmentalists
nor an ecological problem that concerns ecologists
It is not any of those problems in the technological world
but technology's non-technological problem – mathematical
      problem
which stems from technology's very nature of irrepressible
      advance

Technological advance may be able to satisfy
      environmentalists:
it can manipulate the atmosphere to reduce carbon dioxide
Technological advance may be able to satisfy ecologists:
it can bargain with nature to restore some tropical rainforests
But, no matter how advanced technology becomes
it cannot break free from its own mathematical crisis
just as even the greatest force cannot make one equal two
Mathematics is not about technology, but about logic
The acceleration of technology is an illogical proposition

We cannot change mathematics to suit this proposition
so we have to change ourselves, that is
to apply the brake of reason to stop this irrational process
to cease technological competition as we cease the military one
Change the form of civilisation:
replace technological civilisation with an artistic civilisation
Give up the utilitarian system:
replace the value of the market with the value of aesthetics

Close down the particle accelerators –
let nature enjoy nature
Turn scientific funding into literary prizes –
let the arts harmonise life
Let physicists compose music
hearing something that is beyond 'air vibration'
Let chemists write poetry
dissecting feelings and emotions that are finer than atoms!

There will still be flowers of wisdom
and there will still be the pleasure of creation
but artistic civilisation will not accelerate
because art is not a function of time
No poet of today
dares to claim he has overtaken Homer or Goethe
No composer of today
dares to boast he has surpassed Bach or Beethoven
Art is spirit
Spirit is proportion
The ancients' happiness and ours are both happiness
– no greater or smaller
The ancients' sadness and ours are both sadness
– no heavier or lighter

Stopping the competition of technological civilisation
and pursuing the harmony of artistic civilisation
– are these a madman's dream or Utopian?
No, mankind had experiences of non-technological civilisation
Were the Middle Ages in the mist of theological civilisation
for over a thousand years?
It was dark, but with staying power
Was China in the cradle of small-farmer civilisation
for over two thousand years?

It was slow, but in steady cycles
They might not be brilliant chapters of history
but have shown the possibility of
other kinds of value systems and civilisations

We do not need to invite God or emperors back
nor do we need to return to Taoist naturalism
What we do need is to understand that
a great civilisation does not mean we cannot choose –
between the flourishing of cities and the tranquillity of the
      countryside
between 'being rich but tense' and 'being simple but
      harmonious'
between a costly Moon-landing programme
and the fairy-tale of Goddesses' Moon Party
between the scary roar of jets overcoming gravity
and melodious notes from a buffalo boy's bamboo flute!

If we choose an artistic civilisation
it is because we follow reason –
the reason of avoiding destruction
the reason of surviving ourselves
the reason of being free from the slavery of a value system
and the reason of obeying the law of mathematics
Human beings, you unique species blessed with reason
how can you refuse this final wisdom?

9. Epilogue

There was a chicken who lived happily
Every morning, someone opened his coop and fed him
Day by day, month by month
he believed that this was the law of the world
so never thought of escaping
Until New Year's Eve
he found a kitchen knife at his neck
The law disappeared
and it was too late for regrets!

It may be laughable for man to worry that the sky might fall
but it is not laughable for the 'falling sky' to worry about
        man!
The destruction of civilisation cannot be 'known'
Only mathematics, which stands aloof from the world
can sense the storm from the ancient Milky Way
Those who have felt it should ponder deeply over it
Those who have realised it should issue a cry loudly
Be a madman – let others laugh
Laughing is better than being oblivious
as those who are laughing are no longer sleeping!

On the Logic of Love and Marriage

'The more civilised people become, the less capable they seem of life-long happiness with one partner.'

Bertrand Russell's *Marriage and Morals*

Argument

This poetic paper, based on the assumption that human beings covering their bodies was earlier than establishing private ownership, proposes an evolutionary (non-economic) explanation of the origin of the institution of marriage. Marriage was 'the continuation of the fig leaf', in the sense that it restrains human nature of polygamy so as to ascertain fatherhood, as evolution required. With the disappearance of the primary necessity of 'ascertaining fatherhood' in modern life (as society looks after every child), culture, which has been separated from evolution process, is leading to the choice between keeping and abandoning the institution of marriage. As this institution and sexual liberalism are mutually exclusive moral systems, society must decide one way or the other.

1. The Question

Never have human beings talked so much about love as today
Neither have they treated marriage so lightly as today
The more love is talked about, the more fragile marriage
becomes
This inverse proportion is almost mathematical –
When the numbers of love stories exceeds half the total stories
the divorce rate is approaching fifty per cent too
When young people use 'sexy' to describe cars and houses
the marriage rate is plummeting as well

Weddings are still jubilantly celebrated
Vows are still seriously made
There are still Royal ceremonies flamboyant as ever:
salvos rumble, awaking the dead resting in the earth
the 100-yard train carries the longings of the girls in the world
But, what's the use, what's the use?
In the end
the rumbling salvos are no more than bells tolling for a
tragedy
the 100-yard train is a thousand handkerchiefs ready for tears
A fair maiden who can love everyone in the world
just cannot love her own husband
A beauty who can be loved by everyone in the world
just cannot be loved by a husband of her own
Is this fate, or the nature of the era?
Modern communication can dismiss time and space
– talking to the Milky Way
but cannot even connect two hearts side by side!

If Yin and Yang have changed, and can no longer unite into one
then where will the great institution of marriage go?
If it ought to end, why did it start?
If it is not destined to end, how will it continue?
The worries of history are culminating at the turn of the century
interrogating guilty men and women
There is no answer – all we can do is to reflect on civilisation
to see what is love, what is marriage
and if there is a way out

2. The Unfaithful Hormones

Sexual love is the emotional extension of sex drive
Sex drive is the instinct of desiring the opposite sex
It is like the urge for food in many ways
but different in others

Sex and eating are both natural needs of the body
They are both about stimulation and both selective
Eating concerns taste, smell, and looks
Sex concerns looks, sound, and touch
Eating can be so enjoyable – hard to stop for many who want to
Sex can be so exciting – out of this world
Appetite is the 'sex drive' of the mouth and stomach
Sex drive is the 'appetite' of the sex organs
So Mencius says: 'eating and sex are human nature'

However, the two are different
because their objects are different
The object of eating is matter
The object of sex is human beings
This one difference changes everything
as it involves emotion, dignity, welfare, and rights
which change the matter from biology into sociology
Thus, the meeting of eyes is called 'flirting'
The pressure of limbs is called 'cuddling'
The exchange of saliva is called 'kissing'
The penetration of organs is called 'making love'
And thus there are inexhaustible problems of love . . .

Oh –

There are so many songs about love that the atmosphere has
    been inflated

There are so many books about love that the earth rotation has
    been slowed

People praise loyal and steadfast love

and condemn those who flit from flower to flower

Undoubtedly, among all the problems of love

the most fundamental one is the problem of change

Sexual love is something that easily changes by its nature

because 'sex' and 'love' are both organic

Zoology shows that animals' sexual desire is not exclusive –

the desire for the opposite sex is not confined to one particular
    object

*Most species are polygamous, except for a few, such as the
    wolf*

Human beings, of course

have come far beyond the general situation of animals

But the nature of hormones remains unchanged

Love is a more complex project – a multidimensional chemical
    space

From attraction and possession in zoology

to appreciation and admiration in aesthetics

from enjoyment and fulfilment in psychology

to welfare and responsibility in sociology

there are so many factors playing their part, and each one
    changes

Moreover, a relationship is bilateral

which multiplies the dimensions of the variable space

In the words of a physicist, love is a 'vector'
with the measures of both size and direction
They both change, and every change brings other changes
In the words of a chemist, love is a 'process of reaction' –
chemical combination and resolution, oxidation and reduction
When people extol 'eternal love'
they are extolling that a chemical process can be
**   unconditional**
– extolling a sheet of iron that won't ever rust
newspaper that won't ever turn yellow
or chicken soup that won't ever turn sour

Of course, changes bring their consequences
When a lover is no longer loved, it hurts
The hurt and hate can be as great as the sky falling in
The Thames is the tears of lost love
The Nile is generations' reviling of betrayers
However, no matter how much love, hate, joy or sadness
what matters most are the children –
All the rivers on the earth merging into one
cannot accommodate the responsibility for future generations
So far, mankind has only one instrument to prevent such
    changes
That is marriage

What were the origins of the institution of marriage
which regulates human sexual activities?
This is difficult even for anthropology to answer
as it happened in the too far distant past
However, we can use the logic of evolution to trace it back –
making sense of a history that cannot be repeated

3. Evolution Requires Monogamy

The result of sexual love is progeny
To strengthen progeny is the direction of evolution
When species are in a state of indiscriminate mating
the connections between father and progeny are not realised
Some males have no idea of their own 'progeny' at all
Some cannot tell whose DNA is whose
Without a father's protection, it is hard for the young to survive
So reproduction is 'mass breeding with few surviving'

Human beings also went through 'the age of fatherlessness'
The promiscuous population didn't connect men and children
Babies were thought to be produced by women alone
so fathers and children were not even aware of their being
        related
No one knows how many incidents it took, by accident or
        inevitably
for life eventually to reveal two secrets:
one was man's important contribution to reproduction
the other was that children with fathers survived better
It was these 'models' on the road of evolution
that suggested the direction of sexual monogamy

Some people explain the origins of marriage with economics
as marriage does relate to many elements of property –
not only the transferring of belongings, from dowry to
        inheritance
but also changes of personal ownership
This is true, but if it is believed that
human beings covering their bodies was earlier than private
        ownership

then another question may be more interesting and profound:
why did human beings start to cover their bodies –
where does the sense of sexual shame come from?

This is a legitimate question in a comparative study
Human beings have many organs, but why are sexual ones
        shameful?
Human beings have many activities, but why are sexual ones
        embarrassing?
If it is a natural reaction, why does it not apply to animals?
Animals are not ashamed of their sexual organs or activities at
        all
The monkeys in the zoo scratch their genitals in public
just as they scratch their noses or ears!

Christianity uses the mysterious 'forbidden fruit' to explain this
as the beginning of the complicated relationship between God
        and man
It is not very convincing, but shows how important the issue is:
a fig leaf led to the whole of history!

The theory of evolution provides a more objective explanation:
evolution requires 'having a father'
To ascertain a father needs a fixed man–woman relationship
Such a relationship needs to be symbolised by body covering
– certain parts of the body are only available to a certain
        individual
Therefore clothes are worn, bringing with them the mystique
        and shame of sex
Monogamy needs the support of a moral structure
while morality needs a sense of shame as its foundation
This is why these parts are hidden from view
even though their existence is obvious to everyone

Society developed along this road, and reached the institution
     of marriage
Thus, marriage is the continuation of the fig leaf!

The institution of marriage can be of one husband and one wife
or one husband and more wives
but rarely of one wife and more husbands
This asymmetry is not 'sexual discrimination', as some may
     think
but the biological restriction of the purpose of marriage:
'one' husband can ascertain fatherhood, while 'more' can't
Ascertaining fatherhood is a requirement of evolution
and so the mission of marriage

4. The Good and Evil of Marriage

Marriage is a social institution to fix a man–woman
*   relationship*
It is a 'self-cocooning' unprecedented in the history of
*   animals*
This cocoon is both a fortress and a prison:
outsiders cannot get in, while insiders cannot get out
From the symbolism that is sought from the hardest diamond
and the prayers that are sent to the eternal divine
there is no doubt that the function of marriage is 'prevention of
          change'
To prevent a changing thing changing, social pressure is needed
which includes law, morality, religion, and convention
Marriage is a combination of all these forces

The gravity of a wedding is the heaviness of the yoke
The solemnity of the vows is the heartlessness of the contract
The watchful eyes of the congregation
are piercing swords forcing you never to turn back
The ringing of wedding bells
are to notify heaven and earth what has been said
The pure whiteness of the bridal gown
is to remind you of the sinfulness of making a stain
The magnificence of wedding music
is to suppress all possible distracting thoughts
All these are to prevent change
– a yellow card warning before the game starts
Thus the famous saying:
those who yearn for marriage should not get married
those who are scared of it are more qualified for it!

If sexual love changes by nature, how can 'prevention' be
    possible?
Possible, because human beings are animals that can be
    civilised
Civilisation cannot prevent human nature
but can use some parts of it to overcome some other parts
Man naturally loves to be idle and hates work
but also naturally fights for survival
Thus the system of encouraging work generates industrious
    people
Man naturally tends to pick easy jobs and shirk hard ones
but also naturally wants to succeed
Thus social competition creates fighters daring to compete
Man is naturally inconsistent in love
but also naturally treasures his family and reputation
Thus the culture of marriage has made many lasting marriages
This culture is based on man's ability to conform to two things
One is morality, and
the other is the emotional bond of a blood relationship

Marriage turns love into a moral commitment
bringing sexual love onto the balance of conscience
Love carries loyalty, and sex carries duty
Words bear credit, and actions bear dignity
When hormones and sense of shame work together
man becomes a non-animal animal!

Marriage makes love the emotional bond of blood relationship
When the product of sex connects two streams of blood
the feeling of extending life is shared
not only from the two parties towards the child
but also mutual by 'circulating back' through the child –

I am part of you, and you are part of me
The passion of heredity is overwhelming
The tie of family is both firm and sufficient

However
there are many sufferings in marriage, as well as marriages of
    suffering
Not to mention hundreds of thousands of other reasons
the fading of the flower of love alone makes marriage a dried
    well
From ancient times to today, the well has stifled much stirring
    of love
How much suffering of estranged bedfellows has there been?
How many regrets of meeting each other too late have there
    been?
How many have been humiliated for love?
How many have lost their lives for love?
Extramarital affections are affections as well
Love of a 'third party' is love too
Human beings are the king of the animal kingdom
but they cannot be free to love as a dog or pig can!

In the world of love
there are wronged souls of many generations
Good is with marriage, and evil is with marriage
If the essence of marriage is to protect children
the essence of the essence is a necessary sacrifice

5. Revolution and Retrogression

When civilisation entered the century that cares more for
       humanity
people started seeing marriage as repression from tradition
Sexual desire is a human desire, and human desire is human
       nature
So, rebellions raise again the sword of the Renaissance
and the banner of the Enlightenment
and launch a revolution which is more profound than any
       political revolution
It intends to clarify the relation between man and monkey
and to reclaim something that is important to both of them

With its powerful trilogy
this revolution has dismantled the trinity of 'love–marriage–
       reproduction'
The first step is a step of law: the permission to divorce
which redefines marriage – marriage not for life
(A cancellable marriage is a law that can be broken!)
The second step is a step of society: the recognition of
       cohabiting
which separates love and marriage – love without marriage
The third step is a step of technology: the use of contraception
which separates love and pregnancy – love without
       reproduction
In this way sexual love becomes independent
Love need not be forever, nor does sex need to be monogamous
This has had both the approval of law and the support of
       science

Plus the great guidance of Freud, who has just awakened from a
     'dream'
the era of sexual liberation begins

From the 50s to 90s of the Twentieth Century
Britain's divorce rate rose by 600 per cent
Non-marital cohabiting has become common practice
Extra marital affairs have been defended by philosophy
Bertrand Russell wrote his famous *Marriage and Morals*
to analyse human nature with a mathematical logic
He believes that marriage is for children rather than love
but love is precious so it should not be constrained by marriage
Therefore he advocates overcoming jealousy and tolerating
     adultery
so as to liberate sexual love while maintaining marriage
What a romantic logic
but it forgets that jealousy is the very nerve of love!

Sex has been liberated from tradition, bedroom, as well as fig
     leaves –
changed from something that can only occur but can't be seen
     or spoken of
to something that can be seen and talked about everywhere
Everywhere there are lustful eyes and lips, breasts and legs
Billboard women make love to every man
Licentious music makes bishops lose their heads
Teenage girls who haven't mastered language and grammar
have learned how to talk with their bottoms
Even some Bibles have been re-bound with drawings of the sin
     in Eden
– a naked soul is more sexy than a naked body!
Not to mention the commercial world where it is a matter of life
     or death

who dares not to use a sexy packaging to play on animal
    sensitivity
Porn films have started to pursue Oscars
Lovemaking will soon enter the Olympics . . .

Tradition, of course, is still fighting on
The Church is still pushing the spiritual life
The Government is still urging family values
Men and women of honour are still condemning adultery
and still not allowing their children to watch late-night films
The Twentieth Century is a battle field of two moralities
The institution of marriage and sexual liberalism are in combat
    everywhere
The former talks about fidelity, family, and responsibility
The latter talks about sex, freedom, and 'the here and now'
The two values in opposition are offsetting one another
Society is in the state of 'wave-particle parallelism'
– full of hypocrisy

When hypocrisy is defined as civilisation
'civilisation' displays its skill to the full
There are priests who abuse children under the sacred light of
    God
There are presidents who share chairs of power with prostitutes
There is even DNA evidence
showing that those beautiful words about family values
are either gaps between obscenities or the sleep-talking of
    licentiousness
Oh, even people who used to be over-critical have become
    tolerant
Because it has been such a common sight
that they are now able to put themselves in his shoes

Letting an adulterer be the president makes their own
       adulteries tolerable
whether in law or in conscience
Letting a liar be the president makes their own lies tolerable
whether in conscience or in law!

This is revolution or retrogression – who dares to conclude?
If eating and sex are two basic needs of human beings
then human development has not got them balanced
The rise of productivity and the restriction of marriage
seems to have made the population well fed but 'semi-starved'
       for sex
Rebellion of the starving is inevitable
– who can say it is not a revolution?
However, morality is so relative:
compared with the oppression of the past ten thousand years
it is revolution
while compared with the revolution ten thousand years ago
it is retrogression!

6. *Morality Relies on Logic*

If marriage is the price of man's evolution
today there are two choices
We can take human development as the priority
– sticking to the institution of marriage
and continuing to sacrifice ourselves by restricting sexual
          freedom
Or, we can take our happiness as the priority
enjoying sexual freedom by giving power to the condom
which can both control reproduction and prevent AIDS
As far as value is concerned
no one can prove which way is 'more' correct

But society must have a consistent logic of morality
If it is of restricting sex, then not of indulging sex
If it is of indulging sex, then not of restricting sex
If it is a morality of marriage, then not a morality of sexual
          liberalism
If it is a morality of sexual liberalism, then not a morality of
          marriage
This is not dogmatism, but formal logic
Logic is something harder than stone!

Islam's asceticism is a logical system
Since being ascetic, it is reasonable to dress women in veils
It sounds terribly rigid, but is logically consistent
Western permissiveness is also a logical system
Since being permissive, why shouldn't one strip off and sleep
          around?
To die for love, isn't AIDS also a kind of glory?
In comparison

the equivocal official liberalism of today is not a logical system
**To claim family values in an environment flooded with ads of
    nudity
is to have a bath in mud, or to cultivate chastity in a brothel!**

If we are to stick to the institution of marriage
the law of marriage must be obeyed
Only when sex before marriage is forbidden, will people enter
    marriage
Only when divorce is as difficult as rising to the sky
will people try hard to make marriage work on the ground
Only when porn performances are banned
(including the seduction of fashion and makeup)
will men be able to content themselves with their wives' limited
    beauty
Only when 'third parties' and extramarital affairs are punished
will it be possible to protect marriage and the family

'What an extreme view!' – modern man cannot help but cry out
But aren't extremes the very mechanism of marriage?
Combining two into one, the 'war of love' will be full of woes
If it is not driven
there won't be enough momentum to sustain it
If the retreat is not cut off
there won't be enough resolution to move forward
(If people are allowed to change their minds, the minds will
    change
Just as Sunzi said in *The Art of War*:
'Drive them into a fatal position and they will come out alive')

On the other hand, it is also possible to abolish the institution of
    marriage
and simply take the way of sexual liberalism

Unrestrained, how much desire and admiration can be
          materialised
Free and easy, how much love and excitement can be enjoyed
Problems of children there may be, but today is no longer the
          past
The welfare state has taken the responsibility for children
The state is 'the father' of those single parent families
The new generation of women doesn't care about having a
          husband or not
They dare not marry, and dare divorce –
They stride proudly ahead
holding one, carrying one, and bearing one!

If sex can be free from marriage
there is no reason why it cannot be free from fig leaves
Russell has shown that
human beings can dispel the sexual mystique by practising
          nudity
so as to dispel sexual fear and oppression
In that pure and transparent new world
sex will become as natural and ordinary as eating food
So natural and so ordinary – making love is like shaking hands
There will be no pornography for police to clear up
and the profession of prostitution will no longer be needed
Although fidelity may have been as laughable as foot-binding
no one will be perplexed by lawsuits of divorce anymore
Lovers can get into bed as well as get out of it
The 'demand' will create a thousand new medicines for AIDS

Morality is a way, and a way is a logic
Logic means the law of excluded middle:
A and non-A may both be OK
but it must be one way or the other!

7. Concluding Remarks

From the charming tale of Adam and Eve covering their bodies
to the modern scene of nudity on Brighton Beach
the history of civilisation seems to have proved Hegel's
       dialectics –
from undress to dress, and back to undress
But the further profundity of history is the farewell to Darwin's
       Evolution –
it shows how evolution and culture have become separate
       things:
evolution determined the development from undress to dress
while culture has led mankind to face the choice between the
       two again
Being dressed requires the morality of being dressed
Being undressed requires the morality of being undressed
When nature can no longer navigate
logic becomes the compass of morality!

On Reason and Religion

Argument

Since religion is the belief in something important but beyond proof, it forces reason into a paradox: if we are rational, we should always believe in God; but if we are rational, we would never know how to do so. In other words, those who don't believe haven't attained reason; while those who believe have lost their reason.

1. The Guessing Rule of Reason

Religion is the belief in something beyond proving
The existence of God, heaven, hell
can neither be proved, nor disproved
Taking the unprovable for disproof
is to say non-white is black
Taking the undisprovable for proof
is to say non-black is white

For things that are beyond proving
how should reason make its guesses?
Religion says 'believe there is, then there is'
Science says 'no proof, no belief'
But when I invite reason to judge
surprisingly
the religious position proves the more scientific

Reaching this conclusion
is because reason has two functions
One is to distinguish between truth and falsehood
– in the sense of knowledge
The other is to assess gains and losses
– in the sense of expediency
When things cannot be proved to be true or false
the guessing rule of reason is to weigh the pros and cons

For instance, in the modern judicial system
there is a rule called 'assumption of innocence'
When a person can neither be proved guilty, nor innocent
the law assumes he is 'innocent'
Because according to scientific calculations

to have such a rule is more beneficial –
Although some criminals may escape punishment
as far as maintaining confidence in the law is concerned
preventing wronging the innocent is more important
Whereas
when a convalescent who cannot endure the cold
reads the floating clouds before stepping out
his reason should assume it will rain
He should take his rain apparel to be more safe than sorry

This guessing rule of reason
is also the ground for having religion
If
believing means the possibility of going to heaven
but also, of course, the possibility of wasting time
while not believing means the possibility of going to hell
but also, of course, the possibility of saving time
then
reason should calculate which risk is more worth taking

If a man spends one day a week going to church and praying
that would be 52.1 days a year
If he worships for 70 years during his life
that would be 3,650 days in all
which is equal to 10 years' time –
10 springs and 10 autumns, 10 years of precious life
But it is insurance for the future
If there is heaven
it would be the ticket for eternal happiness

If there is no heaven
this would be a waste of 10 years' time
But 10 years are merely 10 years

– a little bit more than one tenth of a limited life
Some say 'life is too short to afford to pay it'
But isn't it because life is too short
that one cannot afford not to pay it?
If there is hell
who can stand the unlimited number of 10 years there?

This is simple arithmetic
– even a myopic pedlar knows
he should pay some money to get insured
Surprisingly
although the modern insurance business is thriving
attendance at modern churches is declining
I believe this is a language problem
If churches are renamed 'Future Insurance Company'
won't rational modern men about-face dramatically?

As we can see
reason lies not necessarily in the confident wrinkles on
          scientists' brows
but possibly in the serene smiles on the faces of Christians
Religion is a kind of reason
– a science of guessing by the rule of reason
In this sense we may say
to have religion is more scientific
to have no religion is less scientific

2. *If God Does Not Like Religion*

When I argued the reason for having religion
a basic assumption was implied – 'God likes religion'
This seems self-evident, no need of proof
But in fact, it cannot be proved
Therefore, there is another danger –
If God does not like religion
religion could be further away from God than we are

Saying 'God does not like religion'
is like saying a woman does not like being beautiful
It sounds strange but is not impossible
Some women believe beauty brings them misfortune
It is also possible for God to view religion negatively

For example
God may wish not to be discovered
so He chooses not to reside on Earth
While religion keeps talking about His existence
which not only divulges His secret
but also denies His mystery as God
Ironically, it is those who do not believe in His existence
that are the demonstrators of His mystic power

He may also dislike being prayed to
The endless chanting of millions
not only leaves Him no peace
but also implies He is not trusted –
If He is infinite love
why would we need to beg for His care?

If He is omnipresent and omniscient
why would He need the advice of mere mortals?

The principle of religion is that God is different from us
but religion always imagines God from our experiences
We like to be praised, so we praise God
We like big houses, so we build churches
After all, God has our joy and anger
We have His smiles and tears
***What runs through God's veins
is the blood of human beings!***

It is because we have different experiences
that we have created different kinds of God
It is possible that one of them is right
but more likely that all of them are wrong
Therefore
no matter how sincere reason would like to be
its road of pilgrimage winds as a question mark –
***May the distance between God and 'the God' we imagine
be greater than that between God and us?***

Philosophy can never answer this question
Two hundred years ago
Konigsberg's Kant launched his famous war of reason
He wrote *The Critique of Pure Reason* to dismiss God
by disproving 'the three proofs of God's existence'
and wrote *The Critique of Practical Reason* to invite faith back
by proving 'moral law needs God to exist'
But neither half gourd could be complete –
Disproving the proof of God's existence didn't prove His non-
          existence

Nor did proving that we need God prove that God needs
      religion
No philosophy can tell
if religion is directing us to follow God
or directing God to follow its doctrines!

3. *The Conclusion: a Paradox*

Reason's conclusion on religion
is a hopeless paradox –
If we are rational, we should always believe in God
But if we are rational, we would never know how to do so
In other words
those who don't believe haven't attained reason
while those who believe have lost their reason

This paradox is unsolvable
because it stems from reason's very nature
Just as only the blind can see others' fortunes*
the reason that tries to sober up the world
must be a drunkard itself –
It always pursues what it cannot obtain
What it has obtained is not what it pursued!

* In China, fortune-telling is a profession of the blind.

On the War Between Liberty and Equality

Argument

Since the French Revolution, liberty, equality, and fraternity have been the values of modern civilisation. Ironically, the problem of the Twentieth Century is that the conflict between pursuing liberty and pursuing equality has led to war rather than fraternity. Should we allow liberty to create inequality, or should we pursue equality by restricting liberty?

The war between liberty and equality is a war between good
    and good
A war between good and good differs from that between good
    and evil
As there cannot be a winner or loser
it will never end

Liberty is the soul of human beings
When Patrick Henry says
'Give me liberty, or give me death'
he is comparing something beyond comparison
– the value of all values

Equality is the conscience of society
When Abraham Lincoln says
'I don't want to be a master, just as I don't want to be a slave'
he is defining something beyond definition
– the axiom of all axioms

These two wheels of the chariot of democracy
are the air and sunlight of modern civilisation
Sunlight warms air, and air softens sunlight
but, on the other hand
air carries water, and sunlight bears fire
It is this fire–water incompatibility
that has split the Twentieth Century

Someone has proved that
even the greatest revolution cannot make free men equal
because freedom means DIFFERENCE
If you redistributed wealth to equalise a society
freedom would challenge you in the market
Thousands of fans throw their money at a pop star

willingly making someone a thousand times richer than
      themselves
If you wanted to prevent such inequality occurring
you would have to restrict freedom –
either stopping the star singing
or prohibiting the fans being fans

So people argue
should we allow liberty to create inequality, or
should we pursue equality by restricting liberty?
The two wheels separate and go two different ways
One is called capitalism – freedom first
including the freedom of being poor and being unequal
The other is called socialism – equality first
including being equally poor and equally restricted

Of course, they both claim to serve the good
The capitalist good is the good of freedom
That is to let the rich get richer
until they are rich enough to run charities to help the poor
The socialist good is the good of equality
That is to turn the rich into the poor
until they are poor enough that the poor no longer feel poor

This war between good and good
has exhausted the wisdom of the century
The gloom of the Iron Curtain
and the terror of the Cold War
are all because one good wants to defeat the other
– to prove itself more important
Oh, good versus good
God has been invited to witness the fighting

– to see Adam Smith's 'invisible hand'
battling with Marx's scientific dooming curse!

Society is system
System is regulation
Capitalism is liberty with regulation
Socialism is equality with regulation
Liberty and regulation are opposite poles
– a dynamic state competing for life-and-death
Equality and regulation are overlapping
– a static state without much wind for sailing

The noble value of socialism has no 'surplus'
but a lofty ideal disdaining economic ferments
The rich world of capitalism sees no people
but 'consumers' pushing the stock indices
If socialism is human conscience
then capitalism is human nature
If capitalism is a cardiotonic for socialism
then socialism is an antidote for capitalism

When the West mixes the grit of the Welfare State
into the ruthless mud of capitalism, and
when the East uses the grease of the market economy
to lubricate the clumsy gears of socialism
no one can tell
if it is a cold war between two irreconcilable enemies
or two civil wars of self-conquering
if the fall of the Berlin Wall means liberty won the war
or equality won the peace

. . .

It is because freedom cannot be made equal
that idealism has to make a concession –

pursuing not liberty and equality
but equality in restricting liberty
Just as Rousseau says
'Men are born to be free, but are always oppressed'
The oppression sometimes is too much
and sometimes is too little
as too little for someone is too much for someone else
How to adjust between 'too much' and 'too little'
is the most difficult social chemistry
but the most delicate art of civilisation

If there is God
and He only answers one question
then we should ask Him
what freedom should we sacrifice for equality?
But this is like asking
what kind of hell should be built in heaven?
Wise God, of course, would not answer
If He answered
the Twenty-first Century would no longer need Him!

On the Dead Weight of Democracy

Argument

What can the event of a democracy voting for dictatorship tell us? A system of infinitely increasing problems won't survive forever – this law of mathematics will not yield to the majority. Democracy may be powerful enough to crush all its enemies, but will it be able to overcome the weight of itself?

When Democracy votes for Dictatorship
Reason is dumbstruck
The rekindled ashes are laughing at embarrassed History
'Now I am fire sprung from water, no longer afraid of water
– what other revolutions would you like to waste?'

Democracy has committed suicide
Freedom, at the funeral which is almost for itself
invites awkward Reason to give a eulogy
Reason says ' . . . however
this also shows the greatness of Democracy –
it admits where it is weaker than its opponent
Dictatorship may mean a mad man rules the majority
while Democracy could mean the majority go mad'

No one knows what is being added up in the ballot box
– wisdom or stupidity?
While this wonder of 'water kindling fire'
thoroughly shows how absurd Democracy can be
Democracy is nothing else but 'one person one vote'
– like counting the birthrate
'Majority rule' is bullying by numbers
It means neither freedom, nor goodness

Democracy does not mean freedom,
but a majority oppressing a minority
'All men are equal before the law' is no more than half true –
The legislative process itself had favoured those in the
        majority!
According to the principle of mechanics
to be oppressed by a majority
won't be less unpleasant than by one person

As people have to join the majority to avoid oppression
those in the majority may have also been compelled

Democracy does not mean goodness either
Don't be deceived by the look of the ballot box
which is big and square, appearing to be fair
'Big' enables it to accommodate evils
'Square' makes it easy to confound right and wrong
When the majority fancy gambling
gamblers are regarded as heroes
When the majority are drunk
those sober are seen as abnormal
When the majority decide to wage war
they entertain death with mothers' agony!

Granted that there is some fairness
Democracy is destined to be fragile –
those democracies lacking bread are dying of hunger
those that lack efficiency are dying of exhaustion
those that lack education, like a crowd of uncultured children
are directing flattering politics to dodder along
mistaking funerals for festivals!

Democracy is not a Gospel from heaven
Nor is it a serenade of a dreamland
It is the tracks of a chaotic herd of sheep
It is an average probability of molecules colliding
It is a rough competition of numbers
It is an institution of coercing respect
made for beings who don't respect others
This game of '51 beats 49'
is merely a way out of the stalemate of civilisation!

Is this the Democracy we fought for with our lives?
Yes, and no
We pursued Democracy as we had never had Democracy
So we had a wrong dream, and assumed that
when dark was driven away, what was left must be light
In fact, driving dark away is only driving dark away
– what is left are the problems not seen in the dark!

What is Democracy?
Democracy is all the problems left after Dictatorship is gone
the problem of freedom
the problem of law and order
the problem of the economy
the problem of education
The problems are as numerous as the hairs on a dog
The problems are as chaotic as tangled hemp
Democracy is the right for everyone to contribute problems
Democracy is a great machine for producing problems!

When Democracy decides to have freedom of speech
there comes the problem of abusing this sacred right
the problem of libelling others
the problem of deceiving the public
the problem of inciting racial hatred and religious conflict
the problem of advertising violence and pornography
Once Democracy tries to exert control
there comes the problem of gagging opinion
the problem of media discontent
the problem of human rights
the problem of foreign criticism
the problem of international tension
etc., etc.

When Democracy decides to have freedom of marriage
there comes the problem of the fall in marriage rates
the problem of the rise in divorce rates
the problem of single parent families
the problem of youth crime
the problem of drugs
the problem of AIDS
the problem of the rights of the HIV carriers
etc., etc.

Problems have the infinite ability to produce more problems
Every solution is another production
The wisdom of dictatorship is to prohibit problems from arising
– like a sealed cylinder without oxygen for chemical reactions
While Democracy is an open chemical space
– an uncontrolled chain of nuclear reaction
It is its very nature
to generate many more problems than it has solved!

Democracy expects the law to deal with problems
This is both underestimating human creativity
and over-estimating what we can endure
In the modern age
the amount of human activities are exponentially increasing
and the amount of problems are uncontrollably exploding –
There has been so much legislation that
we have to make indexes for the indexes
and to find lawyers for the lawyers
while the parliamentary legislation machine
is still running round the clock
At such a pace, two hundred years later
half of the population would have to be lawyers

and the other half would have to be policemen
This is not a joke
but the destiny of our great Democracy!

A system of infinitely increasing problems won't survive
        forever
This law of mathematics will not yield to the majority
Democracy may be powerful enough to crush all its enemies
but it won't be able to overcome the weight of itself
Democracy is troublesome, is expensive, and is tired
When it is too tired to carry its own fairy tale
it will have to invite Dictatorship to help
Thanks to the accommodating ballot box
which is open to anything!
When Democracy votes for Dictatorship
who dares to accuse the elected of being undemocratic?

. . .

Like a bride being doted on too much
but, in fact, it is a heart split by too many vessels
It has gone – no matter how much love there was
It may be back, being lost makes it attractive again
However, then we will have realised
it is something that may go
just as it may come!

Addendum: Questioning the Referendum

1. Questions and Assumptions

Britain is completely split by the issue of the single currency
but unprecedentedly united over the way of resolution
All the parties and the whole nation have agreed
that it must be settled through a referendum
'Let the people decide'
This is a voice that no one dares to challenge

I respect British democracy very much
but there are two questions like a fish-bone stuck in my throat:
Is it true that people always understand their own interests?
Is it democracy to vote on things the voters don't understand?

The legitimacy of parliamentary politics lies on an assumption:
the parliamentary parties can represent their electors
This assumption is generally true but not always
For some controversial and important issues
the views of electors may not be along party lines
so a referendum is needed to let people speak directly

A referendum is democracy in its highest form
The 'directness' gives it absolute authority
However, a referendum implies another assumption:
'the people understand their own interests'
This assumption is as sacred as a religious doctrine
but is this always the case?

2. If the People Don't Understand

Democracy requires two elements
One is equality – everyone has the right to vote for his/her own
        interests
Two is knowledge – voters should know what their interests are
Because only those who understand their own interests
would really be able to exercise their right to vote
We do not let children vote
because they don't understand their interests
We do not let mental patients vote
also because they don't understand their interests
To invite people to vote on things they don't understand
is to invite the blind to pick colour or the deaf to judge music

Do people always understand their own interests?
With the dramatic increase in scale and complexity of society
it has to be admitted that
there are issues beyond most people's comprehension
For many unknown things, adults are 'children' too –
sufficient age does not mean sufficient knowledge
It is true that knowledge can be obtained through education
but not all matters can be comprehended with a short course

How would voting be effected by ignorance?
Operational research shows that
if there is a relatively correct choice
the ignorance in voting would reduce its chances
When a thousand people vote on an issue that is only
        understood by ten
the rationality of the ten will be drowned in the sea of ignorance
– one per cent is too little to make any difference!

So, when there are different opinions on a surgical procedure
the hospital refers it to an expert committee
rather than a social referendum
'Expert voting' is also democracy –
People need specialists to help with their voting
just as they need to have their GPs and solicitors

3. 'Not Understanding Is Not Understanding'

Whether Britain should join the single currency
is an extremely complex and highly technical matter
Either way has countless advantages and disadvantages –
many many economic, political, and cultural concerns
many many short, medium, and long term consequences
Some effects may be foreseen, while most are not
An overall understanding takes special knowledge and
        calculation
Even well-trained politicians find it beyond comprehension
This is why parties have been split, regardless of any solidarity
So, isn't it making fun of the reputable British democracy
to ask people on the street to vote on such a matter?
(Some are against the euro for the absence of the Queen's head
as if they would go to war with Scots because they wear kilts!)

If the principle of not allowing children to vote is right
to use a referendum to decide the single currency is wrong
Parliament shirking its responsibility in the name of
        democracy
is a pilot handing over a plane in an emergency to the
        passengers in this name
The matter should be decided by a certain 'expert democracy'
for example, to let a thousand mature economists vote on it
Although this won't guarantee a correct decision
it will be a scientific one rooted in reason

I do not, of course, expect the country to heed my advice
so I leave this poem to those heading for the ballot box
The ballot box is the symbol of modern democracy
but don't forget, its slot should be guarded by knowledge

Democracy with knowledge is equality and power
while a ballot box of ignorance is a political dustbin
Britain did not have Confucius, but can have his words:
'understanding is understanding
not understanding is not understanding'
A rational man shouldn't vote on things he doesn't
        understand
while an abstainer is entitled to be proud of his rationality!

II. On Concepts

On High Heels and Foot-binding

The heel of a high-heel shoe is the binding of foot-binding
It has been the same road under different feet
The **foot**steps of the hundred year women's movement
is merely an aesthetic change from the Chinese to the Western –
turning a compelled two-dimensional restriction
into a freely chosen three-dimensional bending
The social status is raised for a shoe heel
while the price is walking on tiptoes for life
Oh, the ever suffering feet, no matter how innocent you are
the definition of 'feminine beauty' is to deform you
Because this is the base enabling men to stand firmly

How to Prove 'Doctors are Lower than Prostitutes'
The ethics of a fully commercialised society

If we agree on two seemingly reasonable assumptions
we can prove the morality of doctors is lower than that of
        prostitutes
The first assumption is:
in a fully commercialised society everything is a commodity
so all professions are businesses for making money
The second assumption is:
making money from agony and from pleasure are different –
the higher the degree of compulsion, the lower the morality
Then, it follows that a doctor's morality is lower than a
        prostitute's
Because, when a doctor says 'no money, no treatment'
he is blackmailing a person in crisis
while when a prostitute says 'no money, no sex'
she is merely trading goods for goods
So, a man in a white coat is not necessarily an angel
and a tall hospital can be lower than a brothel
Is this strange?
With such ethics of a fully commercialised society
to put someone down you say 'he is worse than a doctor!'

On the Philosophy of Not Showing Dirt

It is said that wearing dark colours won't show dirt
Not showing dirt is regarded as an aesthetic advantage
It is using the weakness of vision
to make objective dirt subjectively clean

If not showing dirt is taken as an advantage
does this mean a desire for being clean?
The benefit of not showing dirt is washing less
so such clothes are usually dirtier

Here, the idea of cleanliness is transformed
into the capacity for enduring dirt –
as long as others don't see it
you yourself can bear it

This means that beauty is an 'overall effect' –
it doesn't matter to be a bit dirty
Life is the art of doing and not doing something
while aesthetics is the perception of this art

On Alienation

Since man put on clothes
his body has become a mystery
When undressing becomes an art
he scares himself stiff

Since man analysed grammar
language has become a mystery
Walking into a class in logic
a storyteller dares not speak

Since man established markets
commodities have become a mystery
Their 'paper tokens' have become king
Their creators are willing subjects

Since man read the Bible
he himself has become a sinner
The taller and larger the Church
the shorter and smaller the believers

This is called 'alienation'
– a unique art of mankind
He uses time to grind history into a distorting mirror
and then scares himself with his distorted image!

On Science

Science divides knowledge into disciplines
Scientists are experts of disciplinary studies
Science uses its own complexity to simplify the world
so that nothing matters any more except itself

As far as mathematics is concerned
the world is merely permutations and combinations
Happiness and suffering are simultaneous equations of history
War and peace are the plus and minus of human beings

As far as physics is concerned
the world is merely a party of molecules
Joy is the jump of electrons
Anger is their getting into wrong orbits

As far as zoology is concerned
the world is merely a flesh-converter
Dining is converting pig's flesh into human's
Reproduction is converting wife's into son's

As far as economics is concerned
the world is merely a market
Learning is a trade between teachers and students
Love is a deal between men and women

As far as psychology is concerned
the world is merely the person himself
It is his dream
in which there is nothing else but his ego

Science uses its own complexity to simplify the world
and performs two miracles at the same time:
it creates man-like machines
and creates machine-like men

Therefore
there is nothing that matters
except science itself
which becomes God of the scientific age!

On Politicians Never Admitting Faults

Why don't politicians admit their faults?
Because people won't let them survive if they do
We tell children that admitting faults is a virtue
but politics shows the greatest fault is to admit one
So the politicians today are like professional thieves
– they define 'fault' as 'being caught'

When Clinton was under investigation for scandal
he asked his Political Advisor:
'Will I survive if I admit it?'
'No, you won't', said the Advisor
'Then, I have to fight', said Clinton
He defeated truth –
being a worthy President of the United States!

Politicians make mistakes just as children do
If forgiveness is mothers' present to children
then 'denying' is the way out the people show politicians
There are no people who don't scold politicians
neither politicians who are not scolded by the people
But, in the age of democracy
are people who scold politicians scolding themselves?

On the Homosexuality Debate

People are debating
whether homosexuality is 'natural' or 'cultural'
This is not difficult to judge –
one only needs to look at animals to assess humans:
Is there mating between a boar and a boar?
Is there kissing between a cow and a cow?
If there is, it is more likely a natural thing
If there isn't, it is more likely a cultural thing
The unity of nature includes human beings

If it is natural, shouldn't we leave nature to be nature?
When an electron changes sex, the atom has to 'divorce'!
If it is cultural, isn't it also easy to understand?
Human beings can be obsessed with many things
from drink and smoke, to ghost and God
Why can't a man fancy a man, or a woman fancy a woman?

The main criticism of homosexuality
is that it separates sex and reproduction
But doesn't the heterosexual also separate many things
that were once together?
Contraception separates sex and pregnancy
Cohabiting separates love and marriage
And divorce, of course, separates husband and wife
Separating pleasure and responsibility
may be clearing up an unnecessary blend of life
just as Kant criticises Plato's view of virtue being knowledge
separating the true and the good reasonably and successfully

On Thinking

For Rodin's **Thinker** *arriving in Shanghai*

It is said that man is the animal that thinks
This is not true
I don't know whether animals think or not
but I do know the crowd often doesn't

From the unifying roar of the Third Reich saluting its Führer
to the wave of the 'red ocean' rolling towards the Red Sun
from rock stars' pretended madness surging into real madness
to Manchester United's football directing the eyes of the world
the crowd is so simple and easy to manipulate
Whether past or present, east or west
whether it is about religion, war, rock stars, or football stars
different kinds of fanaticism are not different!

People can think but don't, because
trends are greater than thought
traditions are heavier than thought
religions are stronger than thought
power is more powerful than thought
A madman's hysteria can be the reason of a nation
A dead dogma can be a movement of society
Oh, a head without thinking
can be filled with anything!

What is thinking?
Thinking is not memory, nor remembering three hundred
        classical poems
Thinking is not longing, nor lingering under the moon light
Thinking is not calculation, nor differentiation or integration

Thinking is not fantasy, nor a dream in the daylight
Thinking is the movement of the Deity –
is the soul of reason pursuing the reason of the soul

As for a trend, it is a cold reef
As for tradition, it is a rude drunkard
As for religion, it is a self-appointed God
As for power, it is the blind seeing nothing
It is the will of water, and the breath of fire
Logic is its iron hooves for galloping through the universe
It may not be difficult to subdue a thinker
while a thought can never be conquered
just as no force can make one equal two!

To think is not man's instinct or necessary function
Without Copernicus, the Earth would still rotate
Without Darwin, apes would still have evolved into man
However, thoughts make the difference between men
greater than that between man and a deity
Kant, who never travelled beyond his hometown of Königsberg
invited God into his heart to discuss 'Practical Reason'
Einstein, as a junior clerk of a patent office
caught up with light to gain eternal life in four-dimensional
        space
Some have never thought throughout their lives –
life owes them a world
While some who have, have created many new worlds!

Today, people are so proud of computers
But even the most powerful software won't make man think
Computers carrying out man's instructions
is merely man executing computers' orders

So there will be a 'Matthew Effect':*
those who think, think more
those who don't, think even less
'The Net' may have caught almost everybody
but the high-performance screen can be more desolate

Someone said that 'when man thinks, God laughs'
But if man does not think, God will be bored
God likes the fun of thinking but not its hard work
so He creates man to do the work for Him
Man has two options:
to think – to be a hard-working God
not to think – to be a relaxed slave
This oldest of Greek issues about thinking
is still the first issue that needs to be thought

* Matthew Effect: 'the rich get richer, and the poor get poorer.'

On Hypocrisy Being a Psychological Toilet

A fierce competition has ended on TV
The loser, however, looks rather cheerful
He warmly congratulates the winner
and the smile on his face is perfect
A boy who has understood the psychology of competition
cannot understand such a facial expression
'Mum, why is he smiling when he has lost?'
'Foolish boy, this is called being civilised'
'Is his smile real or pretended?'
'Well, of course it's not real
He wanted so much to win but failed
His heart must be in tears'
'Isn't pretending to smile hypocritical?'
'Well . . .' Mum finds it difficult to answer
The boundary between hypocrisy and being civilised
is not a line that Mum can easily draw

The problem stems from the use of language:
the word 'civilisation' is a noun
while 'civilised' is an adjective
The noun distinguishes man from animals:
from pretended smiles to atomic bombs, all belong to
　　　　'civilisation'
just as from foot-binding to Nobel Prizes, all belong to 'culture'
While the adjective distinguishes man's behaviour:
to say 'hello' is 'civilised'
to spit on the street is not

However, the commendatory meaning of the adjective
has narrowed our understanding of the noun:

'civilisation' is understood as a 'good thing'
so things that are not good are excluded
This is why Mum could not answer her son's question –
hypocrisy, obviously, is not something good
but it seems to belong to civilisation as well

Being civilised is to break away from man's natural state
For some conditions that cannot be broken away from
certain disguises are needed
Disguises can be material as well as psychological
Toilets are material
Hypocrisy is psychological

Hypocrisy usually takes the form of politeness
Politeness often contains an element of hypocrisy
Anyone who has experienced social life would know that
'How are you' as a street greeting does not mean care
nor does 'Dear' in an ultimatum mean any affection
An opponent's 'best wishes' or 'kind regards'
is only a nice way of saying 'damn you'
This is the duality of politeness:
it is hypocritical to use nice words which are not meant
but it is civilised manners to say unpleasant things nicely

Hypocrisy does not belong to hypocrites but to society
Human nature makes it a golden rule with eternal value
People love as well as hate hypocrisy
but the hate is rational, while the love is instinctive
For instance
it is more likely for a man with ugly looks
to prefer flattering lies to the truth
Vanity, as a psychological state
is more commonly addictive than tobacco, alcohol, or sex

– so common that society has to recognise its legitimacy
as a psychological need to be protected by civilisation
'Being civilised' means being mindful of the eyes of others
Indeed, as far as many civilised people are concerned
the eyes of others are their world!

Therefore, Mum should tell her son
civilisation includes hypocrisy
just as a city includes noises
Hypocrisy is a psychological toilet
just as a toilet is civilisation made of bricks and mortar
An unglamorous need is a need as well
and so that man differs from the monkey
The monkey needn't pretend to smile
while society cannot do without putting on an act

Seeing It, I'm Blind

On 16 February 1996, the supertanker *Sea Empress* struck
a reef off the coast of West Wales, and 100,000 tonnes of Arabic
oil joined the Atlantic ocean.

The slave trading fleet of the Eighteenth Century
forced a plot of Africa into America
mixing up black and white – sowing the enmity of 200 years
The industrial civilisation of the Twentieth Century
has just pushed a piece of Arabia into the Atlantic
injecting oil into water – planting further man-nature hostility

Oh, the tourists of the world, how can you not come
to enjoy the great scene of raping the sea?
The confident rays of the eastern rising sun are hesitating
– not recognising their perpetual destination
The sentimental clouds in the western sunset are puzzled
– where is the handsome lover of yesterday?
Oil, of course, is lighter than water
but heavy enough to suffocate millions of fish
The gulls have broken their strong wings
as they can't lift the mud of civilisation

The environmentalists are rescuing a few birds here and there
but this is worse than doing nothing
Because it creates the false impression
that the earth is being looked after by someone
In fact, it is not
The modern value-coordinate takes the Earth as its 'original
     point'
so the original point itself has 'zero' value in the coordinate

The muddy oil-water is the vomit of nature
– throwing up all the pride and shamelessness of mankind
Losing the sea is still called 'an accident'
Saying the word 'sorry' – just like losing a hat
Accident? No!
Thirty years ago perhaps, but today it is a crime
We know that if it can happen it will
but we pretend we don't know this 'law'

Of course, please forgive us for our bad sight
We can't see the air suffocating in the passionate kisses of
          waste gas
'til the moans of lung cancer patients have drowned the motors'
          roar
We can't see the land struggling in our 'chemical laboratories'
'til we've encountered our deformed cells under a microscope
We can't see the rivers wailing in the thunder of sewage pipes
'til today, we are witnessing even the sea having lost its great
          waves
Seeing it, I realise that I am blind
and feel the chilling embrace of the end . . .

On Love and Religion

When I am in love
it is like worshipping
Longing is the temple
Kissing is Heaven and Earth

When I am worshipping
it is like being in love
Praying is sweet whispering
Enlightening is the climax of the soul

Being in love is deifying the object –
beautifying, privileging, and immortalising
Man and deity attract as opposite sexes
Life is ruthless medium for both

Love needs longing
just as a deity must be distant
Marriage deletes the space
just as there is no religion in Heaven

A deity is an eternal lover
A lover is a temporary deity
So, some who have failed in love
turn to religion, which is nearby

Love plants seeds
The deity becomes seeds himself
The soul is conceived
What follows nine months' pregnancy is faith

On Teeth and Civilisation

According to the design of nature
teeth can last as long as life itself
Losing teeth means death for a tiger
There are no dental surgeries in a forest

But civilisation is making a new law
The more dentists, the weaker the teeth
Toothbrushes and toothpaste enjoy much celebrity
but there are thirty years of tooth-less life!

This is because we have what animals don't
Teeth and chocolate are torturing each other
A part of the body eats another part
Civilisation uses decayed teeth to chew its 'fruit'

Teeth are jade
Civilisation carves
As these 'works of art' have been on display
what are the other 'products' we haven't seen?

On Over-individualism

Some believe that China's 'One Child Policy' is a road towards
individualism that was lacking in traditional Chinese culture . . .

The key difference between Chinese and Western culture
is that between collectivism and individualism
Chinese say 'an individual is a part of a group'
– a bowl will remain empty until there is rice in the pot
Westerners say 'a group is formed by individuals'
– there will be no forest if there are no trees
This difference is deeply rooted, like two blood types
even coagulating the ways of writing names and addresses

Chinese put the family name before their own name
symbolising the group being prior to an individual
While Westerners do the opposite
as they take individuals as the noumenon
Chinese write addresses from bigger items to smaller ones:
country, city, road, house, and person
While Westerners do it the other way round
Westerners put 'I' in capitals, implying the importance of self
While Chinese like to call themselves 'a humble being'
promoting the spirit of 'a little screw in a great machine'

In modern Chinese history
many scholars have advocated Western individualism
But cultural reform is not something for scholars to achieve
Until a sudden 'demographic revolution'
'one child' has taken up the historical mission
The most favourite and indulged generation comes
with the expectations of the world

Oh, every cry is an uncompromised declaration of 'I' –
The sense of the individual leaps over five thousand years
to repay the debts of many generations in one go!
Compared with the Westernisation Movement 100 years ago
it is the revolution of removing the 'dynasty' of big families
Compared with the New Westernisation of changing technology
it is the biological Westernisation of changing flesh and bones
*How could this 'individualism' of monopolising milk not be
     strong –*
it takes smothering brothers and sisters as the cost!

However, over-individualism is not individualism
The real home of individualism is humanism
'Each man's liberation is the pre-condition of all men's
     liberation'*
'I' is his 'him' when he stands at the position of mine†
Human beings are animals with brothers and sisters
Brotherhood and sisterhood are the starting points of caring for
     others
According to the theory of 'social existence determining
     ideology'
there are two possible outcomes of this biological revolution:
acid-alkali neutralisation – forming a proper individualism
or burying tradition – sinking into an absolute egoism

The fundamental problem of human society is 'I am not you'
Individualism is to divide it into two questions to consider:
If I don't think of myself, who am I?
If I only think of myself, what am I?
The unprecedented experiment has yet to be concluded

* Karl Marx.
† Ludwig Andreas Feuerbach.

but the worry of history may not be alarmist talk:
will the unprecedented generation in Chinese history
still be Chinese in the original sense?
Will the only 'one child' of human history
still be a human being in the original sense?

On Ways of Declaring Victory

With the end of the Olympic Games
all nations are declaring their victories
America celebrates its 'No.1 in the gold medal count'
Russia is proud of its 'glorious position as No. 2'
China cheers its 'best record in history'
Britain is happy with 'much better than expected'
There are as many types of victory
as there are ways of declaring it!

This reminds me of some debates in Parliament –
how Government turned problems into achievements
When the Opposition was critical of the recession
the Prime Minister said 'we are better than the French'
When the statistics showed unemployment increasing
the Chancellor said 'the rate of increase is decreasing'

Oh, man has created such a powerful language
which can 'solve' all problems –
can overturn failure in sports
can overcome recession in economics
The only problem that is left is:
are those who listen as intelligent as those who talk?
If they are not, it is the 'wisdom' of wise men
If they are, it is the self-deception of fools!

On the Market and Democracy

When I am purchasing
it is like voting
A good price is integrity
Quality is trustworthiness

When I am voting
it is like purchasing
Support is a deposit
Dissent is disliking the goods

Democracy is about majority
just as the market is about sales
Elections are shopping around
Money is the votes for commodities

The market is democracy of the economy
Democracy is the market of politics
Bargaining is a conference
A resolution is a deal

Politics is economics
because economics is politics
The Peace Prize is from a manufacturer of explosives
because it is business that makes revolutions

On Boxing

The madness of the thousands around the boxing ring
is civilisation's sincere appreciation for barbarity
Hit him! Hit him! Hit him again!
Let the skull be smashed by the heaviest blow
so that the plasma bursts out at body temperature
If the ancient fight between gladiators and lions
had some solemn heroism of competing against nature
then men destroying each other in modern boxing
is only a business of turning blood reeking into profit
But the spectators then and now belong to the same civilisation
– *enjoying others expressing your own brutish nature!*

Roars delivered by language are still roars
Barbarity transmitted by television is still barbarity
Cruelty with regulations is still cruelty
except being more cruel!
When a sport is destroying
the competition is war
All those condemnations of violence and sympathy for the
        injured
including the noble talk of the Red Cross and RSPCA
are merely putting on an act
The seething excitement over the boxing ring has declared
        loudly:
civilisation is a false appearance, as we are still what we were!

On Women's Beautifying

Beautifying is the symbol of feminine civilisation –
a constant re-design and renovation of a given polyhedron
Since most areas cannot be changed
double efforts are made to improve the adjustable parts –
from the unbridled declaration of hair
to the parabola of the end of the nails
The paint of brows and eyes has others' pupils dilated
The lustre of red lips makes the most brilliant words pale
And clothes express the body in the tensest way
generating the fiercest waves of a vertical sea
Still some don't feel enough
so they restore the fashion of a million years ago
to complete the course of back to nature . . .

However, beautifying is women's understanding of men –
every stroke is a molecular formula of an androgen!
They know scientifically (biologically and psychologically)
how a certain colour can hold a vision and imagination
how a certain curve can raise a heart beat and blood pressure
or how a certain shape and size of buttocks
can change the answer to the most important question
as well as the equation of their destiny
Oh, in this over-aesthetic era created by television
beautifying is the most open conspiracy under the sun
Women are struggling in the inflation of sexual value –
using all their understanding of men to understand men
so as eventually to suffer men's 'understanding'!

On 'No Explanation'

Not understanding a text, you ask the author to explain
He refers to some other words, and you thank him
However, if he did have a better expression
shouldn't it have been used in the first place?

If someone says 'I don't explain
This, and only this, means what I meant'
You may find it intolerably arrogant, but
why should the best texts be 'polluted'?

There are writings that are so proper and accurate
that only they themselves can represent themselves
There are also needs for such precision, e.g.
a law put 'in other words' may deform justice

Words can be precise because thoughts can be
Thoughts can be purified and purified, like water
When writing reaches the level of 'no explanation'
it is the water that cannot be washed by water

On Dog and Bone

Western democracy is wondering
why the turn-out for the elections keeps falling?
How could people become so lazy
even unwilling to raise a hand
to enjoy the right they earned with lives?

People are good at inciting political parties to fight
Opinion polls are a juicy bone with political meat
When two dogs are fighting for it, democracy profits
However, in order to get the bone
the dogs make their mouths its shape
The same lip-rounding makes a similar bark
So we can no longer tell one from the other

Once a stable majority has formed
all parties that want to win become one party –
the slave of the majority
So, why bother to vote for 'tea or coffee'?
The withering of electoral interest
means that democracy is 'too' secure
Who is responsible for such 'political impotence'?
The majority!

On the Terrorism of Suicide

When released from the fear of death
men can be MC² times more powerful *
Once they turn their 'mass' into energy
the 'power' is as great as our fear

The terrorism of killing with suicide
is different from that of only killing
Killing is terror
while suicide is a philosophy

Men who don't fear death are dead men
because 'fearing death' is part of life
These dead men invalidate our world, by cancelling
this premise of all laws, norms, and psychology!

They don't fear death, so nothing else
How should these 'living dead' be dealt with?
We may 'talk' to ordinary terrorism with war
but it makes the suicidal one more suicidal

The way to conquer the suicidal
is to make them fear death again
that is to find the reason why they don't
and to invalidate it as a psychiatrist would

---

* According to Einstein's mass-energy relation: $E = MC^2$.

Appendix 1

A Deep Reflection on the Development of Civilisation*
On Chengde Chen's 'On the End of Technological Civilisation'

Fengsheng Guo

Chengde Chen's poetic paper 'On the End of Technological Civili-sation' (*Hong Kong Literature*, 1998,7 and 1998,8) is a remarkable piece of writing, as far as both literature and philosophy are concerned. It uses beautiful poetic language expounding a signifi-cant philosophical issue regarding the fortunes of mankind, and its rigorous and thorough manner makes it both artistically inter-esting and theoretically powerful. Its arguments seem to be extraordinary to the degree of 'peculiar', but are most thought-provoking.

The concept of 'the end' of technological civilisation is difficult to understand for many people. Those who never thought about the issue may be surprised by it: how could it be possible that technological civilisation, on which whole modern society relies and all our expectation lies, is inevitably heading to an end through self-destruction? (As Chen claims in the paper: 'as the nature of technology is to accumulate power of destruction, the meaning of technological civilisation is to accelerate towards its end.') While those who have read some sociology of science may think this is perhaps no more than the technological pessimism advocated by R. Sudre or von Mayer (see *The Science of Science: Society in the Technological Age*, chapter13, edited by M. Goldsmith and A. Machay, Souvenir Press, London, 1964), therefore won't take it too seriously. In fact, reading it carefully, you will find that the

* *Hong Kong Literature*, no. 171, March 1999, by Fensheng Guo, Professor of Philosophy at Shanghai University

question raised and discussed here is neither peculiar, nor repeating an old tune, but refers to a series of underlying theoretical and practical issues which have yet to be touched. The freshness and profoundness of Chen's arguments are not in claiming an end, but in proving a logical inevitability of the end. This is based on two excellent mathematical proofs: the kinematics proof and 'the car-crash theory'. Let's look at the kinematics proof first.

All accelerating processes will end – this is a law of kinematics. Thus far the development of technological civilisation has been an accelerating process – this is also an indisputable fact. If we admit these two points, there is only one conclusion that can be drawn: with such a development, technological civilisation will end. This is a standard logical syllogism, i.e, if we admit the presumption, the conclusion is undeniable. People are surprised, because this 'end' is invisible, intangible, and, indeed, metaphysical. Such an issue won't normally be perceived, and only philosophers who pursue ultimate truth can grasp it.

The other powerful argument is his analysis of the real possibility of 'the end'. The development of technological civilisation has reached the capability of destroying civilisation itself, such as nuclear technology, genetic engineering, etc. The possibilities of self-destruction have been admitted, but we normally believe that these technological possibilities are unlikely to turn into reality. It is believed that human beings share the common goal of survival, so there must be social forces of control to prevent it happening, and technological development itself will provide new means of control as well. Isn't it true that technology has always won the battle of controlling the negative side of its development? It has been a half century since the birth of the nuclear bomb, but we have survived. However, the question for the future is: will the forces of control be so reliable that the world can survive such possibilities forever? This has been debated for a long time, but remains unresolved, because each side can find many reasons, but none of them can be conclusive. 'The car-crash theory' introduced by Chen in this paper is a breakthrough, which provides a decisive conclusion through a mathematical analysis of probability.

A car crash seems an avoidable contingent event, but no driven car can completely avoid such a possibility. According to the theory of probability, the possibility of a possible event, no matter how small the probability, is increasing with the process. As long as the process lasts long enough, the event will eventually happen. Imagine that a man who can live forever drives a car which can run forever, a car crash will definitely happen one day. When technological development has reached the capability of destroying civilisation, isn't it like that car with the possibility of having a crash? If it keeps in this state of development, it won't survive the law of probability forever. If this mathematical logic cannot be overthrown, the only possible reason to deny this conclusion is to speculate that technological civilisation may not be a infinite process. But this is to say that before the car crash happens it may have ended, i.e., with an even shorter life. Compared with the car-crash theory, this theory of 'end' is a speculation lacking grounds.

It is clear that Chen's theory of 'the end' is completely different from the traditional warning theory from environmentalists or ecologists. Environmental or ecological problems are technological problems that can hope to be solved by technological means, while the problem Chen raises is the problem of technological development as a whole, which cannot be solved by technology but only by stopping its development. People may not like this conclusion, but if we cannot refuse its premise and logical derivation, we will have to face the ruthless fact of 'the end'.

It is also clear that Chen's theory is not some kind of doom-theory predicting 'the end of the world'. He logically concludes that technological civilisation with its current fashion of development will end, but does not imply that the world will necessarily have no tomorrow. An accelerating system cannot last, but not necessarily ends in destruction – if the path can be changed. If we are intelligent enough to see the danger and brave enough to change the form of civilisation into another kind, we do not have to end in disaster. Chen has suggested replacing technological civilisation with an 'artistic civilisation', based on the concept that 'art is not a function of time'. I believe this idea can only be regarded as a poet's romantic blueprint, which is inspiring but debatable. However, the issue of 'the end' and of finding a replacement are separate ones. No matter what options of way out we imagine, it won't affect the logical conclusion on 'the end' established by this poetic paper.

Appendix 2

Philosophical Poems as 'Caricatures of Thought'*

Chengde Chen

In ending this book, I explain briefly how philosophical poems can have a place in philosophy as 'caricatures of thought'. Hegel once said 'architecture is frozen music'. How would this poetic expression be compared with a usual academic statement such as 'architecture entails similar aesthetic features as art'? Is it like a concise caricature compared with a realistic painting, being more imaginative, more vigorous, more profound, and therefore more accurate?

Philosophy, as intellectual enquiry, normally pursues truths beyond common sense through rigorous logical analysis, appearing as an abstract reasoning process. Poetry, as a literary form, is normally used for describing feelings or stories presented with images and imaginative language. It is generally believed that the two do not go together because poetic language cannot have the logical rigour that is vital to philosophical enquiry, while the abstraction of reasoning costs poetry its vividness as poetry. However, does the inevitable abstraction of philosophy mean that images should therefore be excluded, or the opposite: that images provide a valuable supplement? The answer is the latter. Looking at how philosophy has been delivered, we can see that many theories are well remembered through vivid images. For Plato's theory of the truth of ideas, we remember the image of the 'cave men' watching shadows on the wall, while for his theory of the reason–will–desire trinity, we remember the image of a 'carriage' with two horses

*This is an edited version of the author's introduction to his philosophical poems published in *The Philosopher*.

and a driver; for the sophist Zeno's Paradoxes, we remember how Achilles failed to catch up with the tortoise, as well as the 'flying arrow' being at rest; for the paradox of set-theory, we remember how Russell's 'barber' became puzzled; for Popper's falsificationism, we remember that one black swan was contrasted with many white ones; for Rawls' theory of justice, we remember how people in 'the original position' were covered by 'the veil of ignorance'; etc.

The importance of an appropriate image to an abstract theory cannot be overestimated. Like images, imaginative language is also not only acceptable but indispensable to philosophical thinking. It is those well-refined and imaginative expressions that are most memorable in philosophy, such as Pythagoras' *'All things are numbers'*, Protagoras' *'Man is the measure of all things'*, Descartes' *'I think, therefore I am'*, Kant's *'Man is an end'*, and Nietzsche's *'God is dead'*. Do not such powerful expressions give the impression that philosophers are poets?

If poetic language is not an enemy but an ally of philosophy, can poetry be used for writing philosophy? Poetry is a powerful literary form that can do many things, from expressing love or declaring war to advertising toothpaste (some say that the best of modern poetry is in advertisement – this is not entirely a joke). The tradition that poetry does not engage in reasoning is based on the understanding that logical rigour and poetic vividness undermine each other. But, does poetry have to be image after image, all the time, so as to exclude reasoning? There is no such literary rule, and what is required is that the reasoning involved should be so interesting that it can be appreciated poetically. In fact, the shared interest of pursuing profoundness does provide the potential for poetry to have a good marriage with philosophical reasoning, so as to make poetry deeper and philosophy more lively.

There were philosophers who wrote philosophy through poetry with great success. Xenophanes and Parmenides were two famous ones in ancient philosophy, and the latter's *On Nature* is a very serious philosophical enquiry written as a long poem. So Aristotle, the man who started the scholastic style of writing philosophy, reckons that 'poetry is more philosophical and more worthy of serious attention than history', because 'poetry is concerned with universal truths' (*Poetics*). In the modern age, Goethe was counted as a great poet with philosophical thinking, while Nietzsche was a great 'poet-philosopher' whose poems form an important part of his main contribution *Thus Spoke Zarathustra*. In the Twentieth Century, T. S. Eliot, as a philosophical poet (who was a student of Russell), discussed metaphysics through his very imaginative poems *The Four Quartets*. As for why imagination can help in understanding the world, Sartre has explained it clearly: imagination is an alternative mode of consciousness, and is addressed to the same objects as perceptual consciousness but to these objects 'as they are not' (*L'Imaginaire*). Architecture is of course not music, but the imaginative expression 'frozen music' does tell us a lot about it. This 'unreal perception' is more profound than many real ones, because it is revealed through an 'inner link', which so-called philosophy is about.

My experience of writing philosophical poems has made me believe that poetry can deliver philosophical ideas and make them more powerful. Compared with a philosophical paper, a philosophical poem is usually relatively simple but more striking, somehow like 'a caricature of thought'. A caricature seems not as lifelike as a realistic painting, but in its simplification and exaggeration it highlights features, and so guides viewers to appreciate the essence more 'accurately'. Here are few examples from my poems which illustrate such efforts:

- To show that religion is a man-made institution: *'We like to be praised so we praise God. We like big houses so we build churches. What runs through God's veins is the blood of human beings'*.
- To describe the inevitability that civilisation will include hypocrisy: *'Hypocrisy is a psychological toilet, just as a toilet is civilisation made of bricks and mortar'*.
- To summarise the evolutionary explanation for the origin of the institution of marriage: *'Marriage is the continuation of the fig leaf'*.
- To explain the market and technology through human nature: *'Human beings are intelligent, human beings are competitive. The intelligence of competition is the market, the competition of intelligence is technology'*.
- To reveal psychological similarities between love and religion:

> *'Love needs longing, just as a deity must be distant. Marriage deletes space, just as there is no religion in Heaven'.*

- To state the precision of thoughts: *'Writing can be precise because thoughts can be. When reaching the level of "no explanation", it is the water that can't be washed by water'.*

Why should such writing be taken as philosophy? My reasoning follows.

(a) The issues under discussion are philosophical, in the sense that some hidden conceptual links which are generally significant can be revealed through reasoning. If a poem achieves this, it has accomplished a task of philosophical inquiry.

(b) When there is a tension between logic and literary needs, it follows the principle that logic comes first. It may sacrifice a certain literary attractiveness to maintain logical clarity and consistency (including using the means of definition, proposition, and inference), but never sacrifices logic for literary gains, nor takes advantage of language ambiguity to achieve false reason.

(c) Although reasoning in poetry may not be as rigorous as in philosophical papers, sensible use of poetic language can make it logically sufficient for delivering philosophical ideas. Logical precision is something acceptable within a range, just as, although most philosophical writings are not as rigorous as those written in formal language, (the form insisted on by some logical formalists) they are logically acceptable.

(d) From the literary point of view, I would say that because it is philosophy, it makes poetry. When a poem is arguing philosophy, its literary loss, caused by abstraction, is compensated by the beauty of reason: the forcefulness of logic and the attraction of exploration. A good argument is a strong forward drive – sometimes it can be stronger than a life story or an emotional expression in a lyric poem. With the help of powerful images, metaphors, associations, humour, antithesis, and other rhetorical or structural means of poetry, which are not used in philosophical papers, a reasoning process can be presented beautifully as well as vigorously, though this is hardly a mission for those who lack imagination.

There can be many kinds of philosophical poems, from long pieces of serious investigation on big themes to short pieces of enlightening discussion. In the form of poetry, philosophy can be read aloud and understood; this is most encouraging, as communicability is the aim of my poetic approach to philosophy.